ROCK GUITAR
BY RON CENTOLA PROGRESSIONS

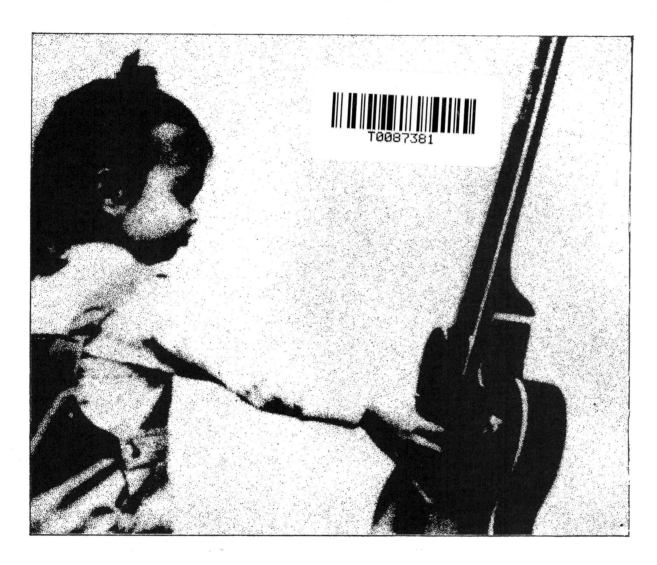

Copyright© 1981 by Ron Centola

Reprinted 2011

To Jennifer
and
Mark

Edited by Anna H. Centola

Many thanks to Gary Centola

Introduction

For the past 30 years rock musicians have relied heavily upon the basic 3 chord rock progression while writing their hits. This book takes an in depth look at the basic 3 chord progressions that have dominated rock songs for so long a time.

As you are playing the various progressions in this book, try singing some of your favorite rock songs. You'll be surprised to discover how many of these tunes are based upon the progressions in this book.

Ron Centola

Special Features

1) Important points to remember are in bold print.

2) You get step by step instructions on how to play each progression.

3) The progressions that are easier to play are presented first.

4) Each 3 chord progression is shown on different positions of the guitar so that you will be able to play that same progression on different frets of the guitar.

5) A special set of rock cards (which easily fit into your guitar case) are included in the back of the book. These cards show you every possible basic 3 chord progression.

Table of Contents

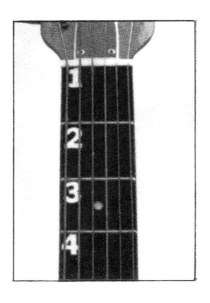

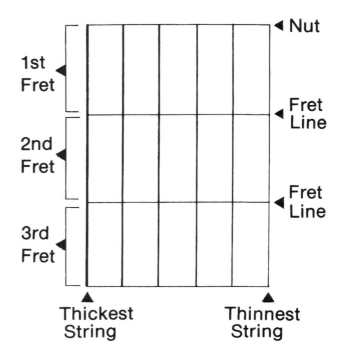

Nut

1st Fret

Fret Line

2nd Fret

Fret Line

3rd Fret

▲ Thickest String

▲ Thinnest String

How To Read Finger Positions On The Guitar Diagram

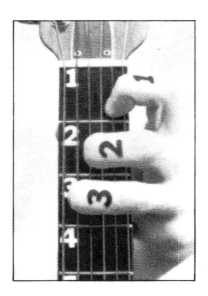

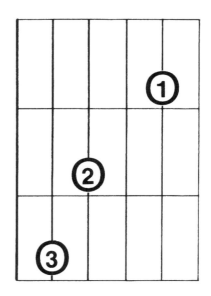

O indicates where your finger is placed on the guitar. The number placed on the circle is the number of the finger used on your hand.

① indicates the **1st finger** on the **1st fret** of the **2nd string**.

② indicates the **2nd finger** on the **2nd fret** of the **4th string**.

③ indicates the **3rd finger** on the **3rd fret** of the **5th string**.

How To Hold A Pick

A Pick

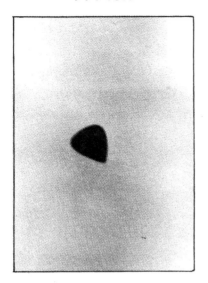

Holding A Pick

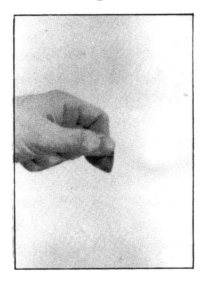

How Your Fingers Are Numbered

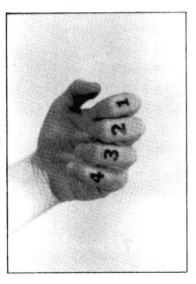

WHAT IS THE BASIC 3 CHORD PROGRESSION?

The basic 3 chord progression is a series of 3 chords that is repeated over and over again in a song.

Learning Progressions

1) You should **learn the finger positions** of the **3 chords** used in the particular progressions you are studying.

2) You should be **able to change** from **one chord to another** in the progression without stopping the strum.

3) You should **master each progression** before you go on to the next.

Student Notes

The (A) Chord Progression

Each progression receives its name from the first chord in that progression. Accordingly, the **G** progression begins with a **G** chord and the **D** progression begins with a **D** chord. If one uses this rule, it is clear that the **A** progression begins with an **A** chord. The **A** chord is then followed by two other chords - the **D** and **E** chords.

The chords of a progression follow a certain pattern. The pattern for an **A** progression is **A**, **D**, and **E**. In other words, the **A**, **D**, and **E** chords will be the only three chords used in a progression.

Learn the finger positions of the chords below.

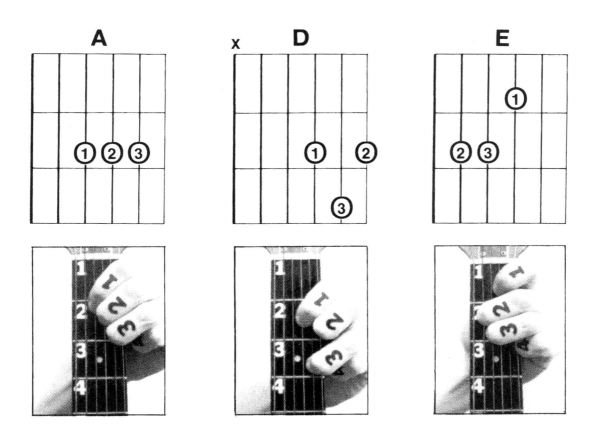

Use the following steps in learning how to play a progression.

Step 1- Learn the finger positions of the chords used in each progression.

Step 2- Learn to change from one chord to another while playing a strum pattern. (See below.)

    a)   Strums-
          1)   A down strum is represented by the symbol (⊓).
          2)   An up strum is represented by the symbol (**V**).

    b)   Strum Pattern-
          1)   A strum pattern is the way the guitarist moves his or her hand over the strings.
          2)   A very common strum pattern is ⊓⊓VV⊓, (down, down, up up, down). An explanation of this strum pattern is on the next page.

Student Notes

Strum Pattern - Down, Down, Up Up, Down
(⊓⊓∨∨⊓)

The strum pattern we are going to learn is ⊓⊓∨∨⊓,
(down, down, up up, down).

1) This strum pattern will be used in the progressions on the
following pages.

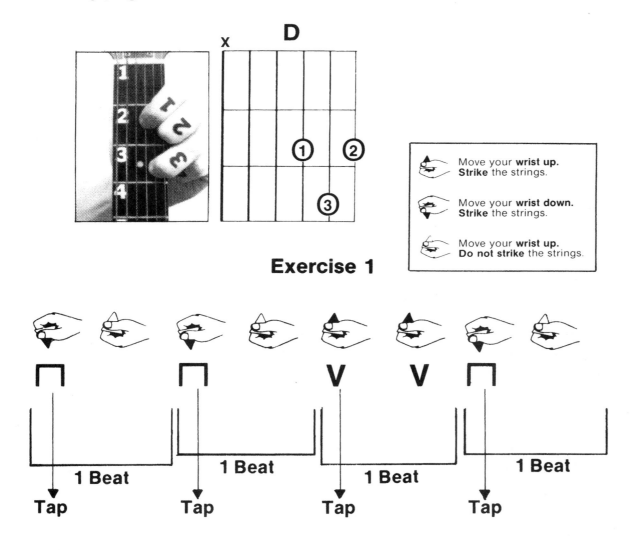

Exercise 1

Move your **wrist up.**
Strike the strings.

Move your **wrist down.**
Strike the strings.

Move your **wrist up.**
Do not strike the strings.

ADVICE

1) **Your hand should not stop** at any point in this strum pattern.
2) The **strum should be continuous,** smooth and unbroken.

Given below is the arrangement of the three chords that make the **(A)** Progression. This arrangement shows you the order that the 3 chords are to be played. It also shows how many times you should play the strum pattern for each chord.

The A Progression

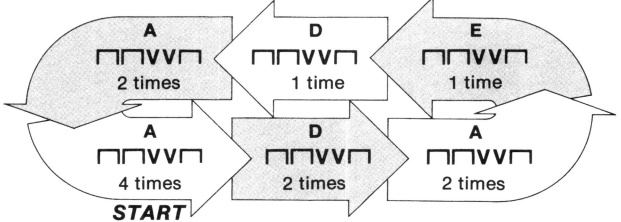

Explanation

1) You **play** the **complete strum pattern** (⊓⊓vv⊓) the **number** of times **indicated under each chord.** For the **A** chord you should play down, down, up up, down (⊓⊓vv⊓) 4 times.

2) You should practice this progression until you can change from one chord to another without stopping the strum. An explanation on how to play the chords without breaking the strum pattern is given on the next page.

3) You have completed the progression when you play the six chord cycle as shown above. You may repeat the progression as many times as you like.

How To Play The Progression Without Stopping The Strum.

Do not stop the strum between chord changes. The strum must be continuous throughout the progression.

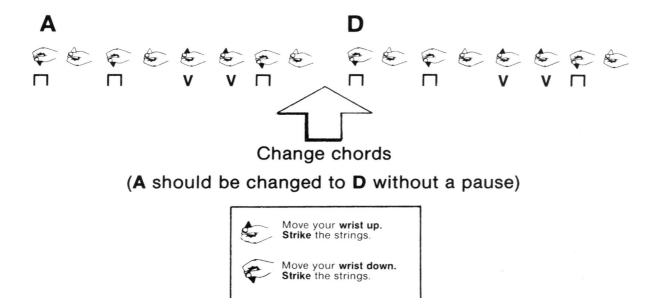

A　　　　　　　　　　　　　　**D**

⊓　　⊓　　V　V　⊓　　⊓　　⊓　　V　V　⊓

Change chords

(**A** should be changed to **D** without a pause)

	Move your **wrist up**. Strike the strings.
	Move your **wrist down**. Strike the strings.
	Move your **wrist up**. Do not strike the strings.

Explanation

1) While you are changing from an **A** to **D** chord your strum should not stop. There should not be any break in the sound.

2) The same strum pattern will be used while playing the progressions on the following pages.

1) You should be able to play the **A** progression clearly and smoothly before you proceed to the progressions on the following pages.

2) While playing the progressions on the following pages you will use only 1st position chords. 1st position chords are chords played on the 1st three frets of the guitar.

MASTERING THE PROGRESSIONS

1) You should **know the finger positions of the chords** that are to be played in the progression.

2) You should be able to **change from one chord to another without breaking the strum pattern.**

3) While practicing these progressions, try singing some of your favorite rock songs. You will be surprised to discover how many of these songs are based upon the progressions that you are practicing.

Student Notes

The D Progression

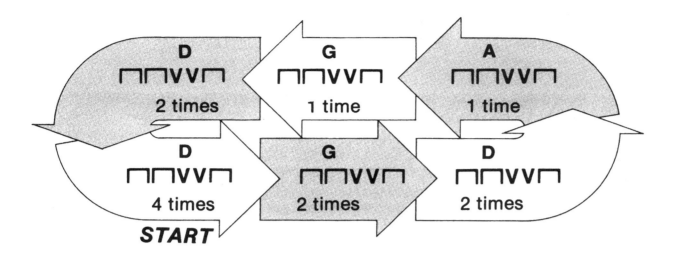

Reminders

1) You **play** the **complete strum pattern** (⊓⊓∨∨⊓) the **number** of times **indicated under each chord.**

2) Do not stop the strum when changing from one chord to another.

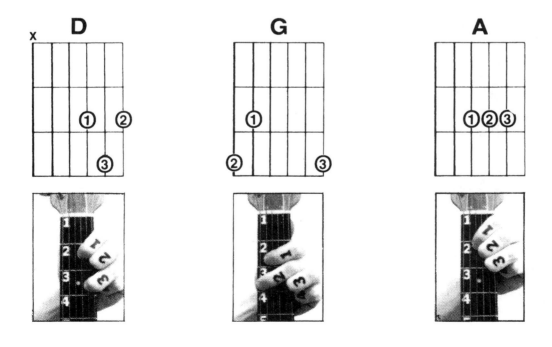

The G Progression

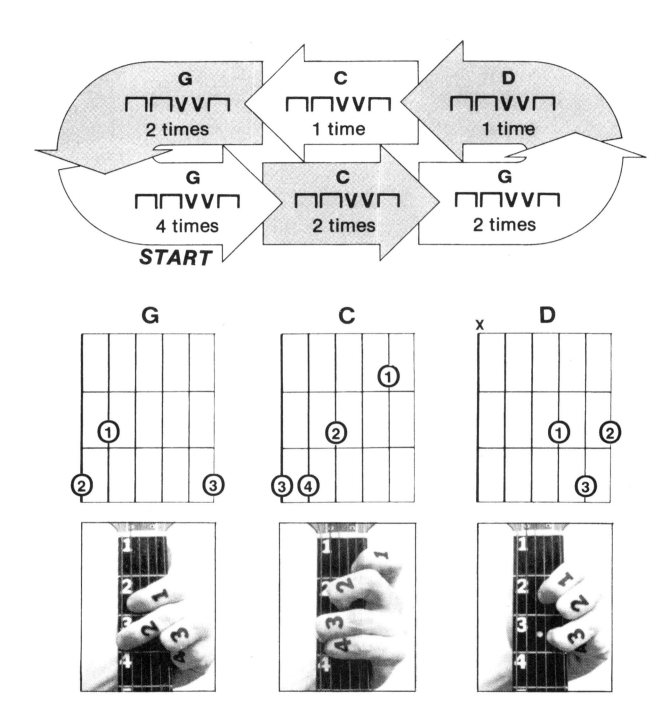

The E Progression

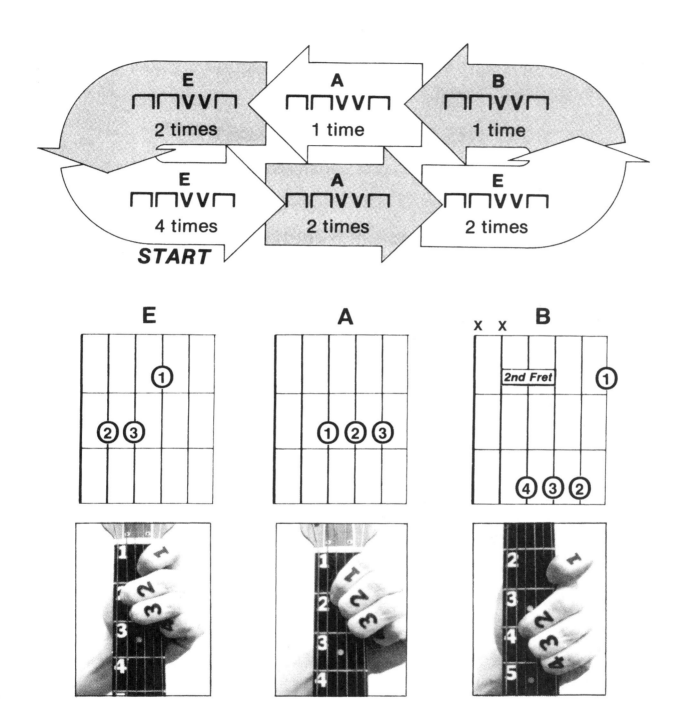

Because of limitations imposed by the musical alphabet there are only 12 possible basic progressions. To understand the musical alphabet you must understand the differences between the musical alphabet and the regular alphabet.

THE MUSICAL ALPHABET

There are two major differences between the musical alphabet and the regular alphabet.

Difference Number 1

A comes after **G** in the musical alphabet.

A   B   C   D   E   F   G   A   B   C   D   E   F   G   A   etc.

The musical alphabet repeats itself over and over again. The fact that **A follows G** in the **musical alphabet** is a very important rule to remember. In the pages to follow, your knowledge of this rule will be very helpful.

Student Notes

Some of the letters of the musical alphabet are separated by sharps and flats.

This is a sharp sign #.
This is a flat sign ♭.

The Musical Alphabet With Sharps And Flats

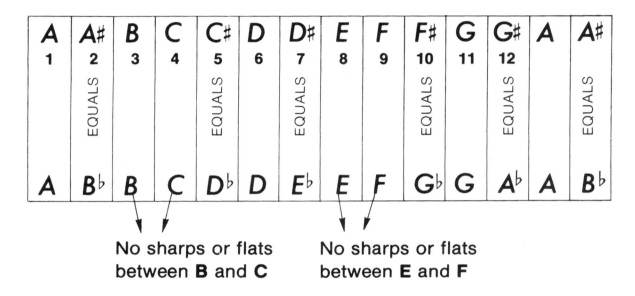

No sharps or flats between **B** and **C**

No sharps or flats between **E** and **F**

Remember, each progression receives its name from the 1st chord in that progression. The possible progressions are:

1	**A** progression	7	**D#** or **E♭** progression
2	**A#** or **B♭** progression	8	**E** progression
3	**B** progression	9	**F** progression
4	**C** progression	10	**F#** or **G♭** progression
5	**C#** or **D♭** progression	11	**G** progression
6	**D** progression	12	**G#** or **A♭** progression

You are probably wondering why some of the progressions have two names. This is explained on the next page.

To sharp (#) a chord you must move it up one fret.
To flat a chord (♭) you must move it down one fret.

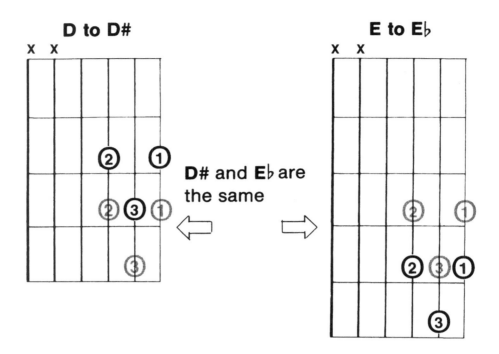

D to D#   **E to E♭**

D# and E♭ are
the same

Explanation

To sharp the **D** chord move the **D** form to the **3rd fret.** Moving it up one fret transforms the **D** chord to a **D#** chord. To flat the **E** chord move the **E** form down one fret. Moving it down one fret transforms the **E** chord to an **E♭** chord. **E♭** is on the **3rd fret. E♭** and **D#** are the same chord.

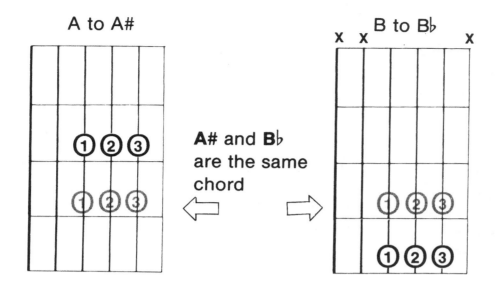

A to A#

B to Bb

A# and Bb are the same chord

RULE: A flat is the same chord as the sharp that is alphabetically before it. Therefore, **Bb** is the same as **A#** - **A** comes before **B** in the alphabet. **Db** is the same as **C#** - **C** comes before **D** in the alphabet **Eb** is the same as **D#** - **D** comes before **E** in the alphabet.

Conclusion

All flat and sharp chords will have two names. Therefore, an **A#** chord is the same as a **Bb** chord.

Student Notes

We will try playing some progressions using sharps and flats. The finger positions used to play the chords in these progressions are more difficult to achieve than those used in the progressions we have already tried.

Playing The Bar Chord Correctly (The F Chord)

Some of these progressions involve the playing of bar chords. While playing **bar chords,** you must **use one finger** to **press down** on **more than one string at the same time.**

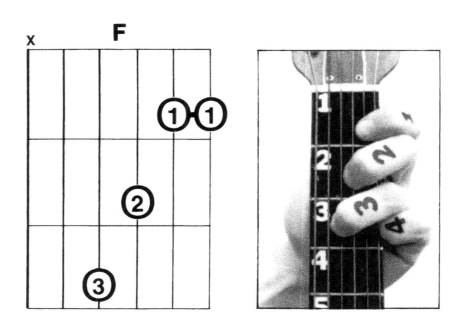

To play the **F** chord you must press down on both the **1st fret** of the **1st string** and the **1st fret** of the **2nd string** with your **1st finger.** Your **2nd finger** should be on the **2nd fret** of the **3rd string** and your **third finger** should be on the **3rd fret** of the **4th string.**

The Right Way   **The Wrong Way**

 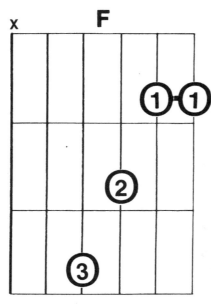 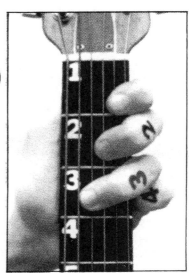

Strings will sound clear.

Your 2nd and 3rd fingers are bent over touching other strings and causing thuds.

More often than not learning to play a bar chord takes a great amount of time. You will probably discover that while playing the **F** chord you must press your 1st finger down causing your 2nd and 3rd fingers to create a thud sound. The only remedy to this problem is practice. Put up with the thuds for a while. They should correct themselves.

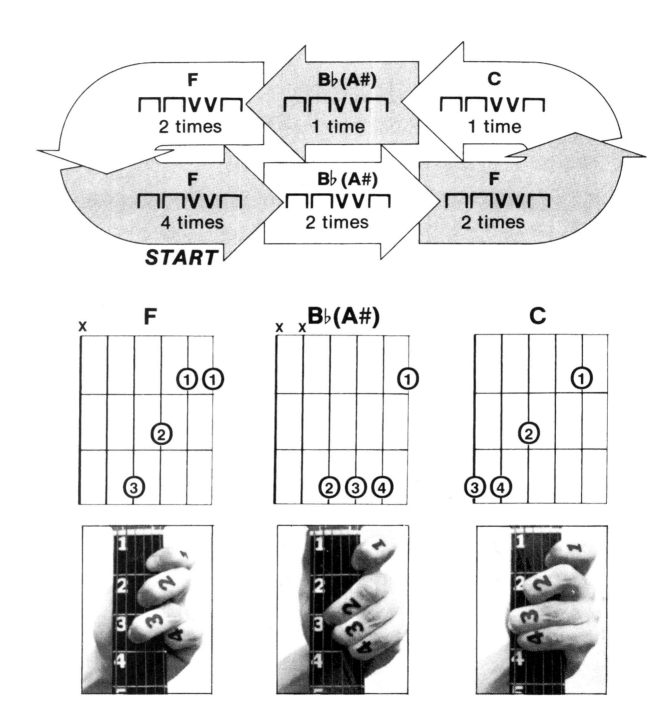

The A# or B♭ Progression

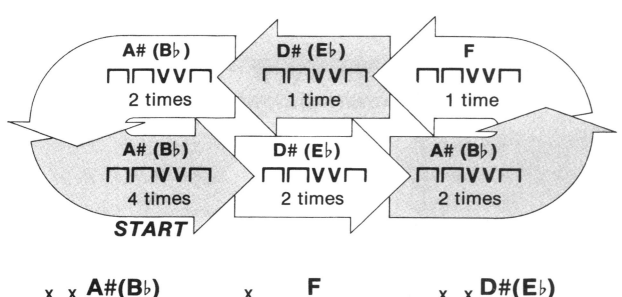

A# (B♭) ⊓⊓∨∨⊓ 2 times

D# (E♭) ⊓⊓∨∨⊓ 1 time

F ⊓⊓∨∨⊓ 1 time

A# (B♭) ⊓⊓∨∨⊓ 4 times *START*

D# (E♭) ⊓⊓∨∨⊓ 2 times

A# (B♭) ⊓⊓∨∨⊓ 2 times

x x **A#(B♭)**

x **F**

x x **D#(E♭)**

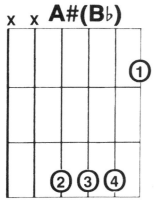
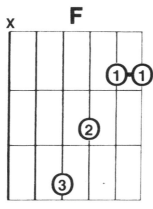
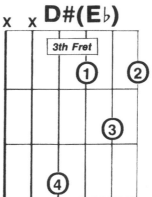

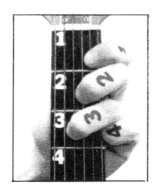
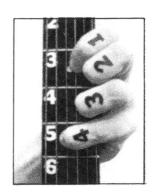

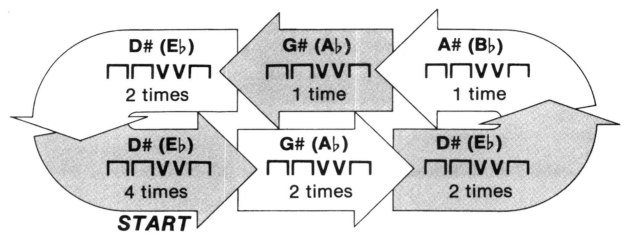

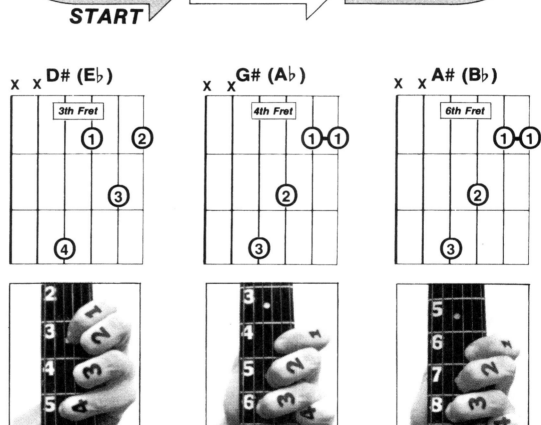

Advice

1) D# and E♭ are the same chord.
2) G# and A♭ are the same chord.
3) A# and B♭ are the same chord.

The F# or G♭ Progression

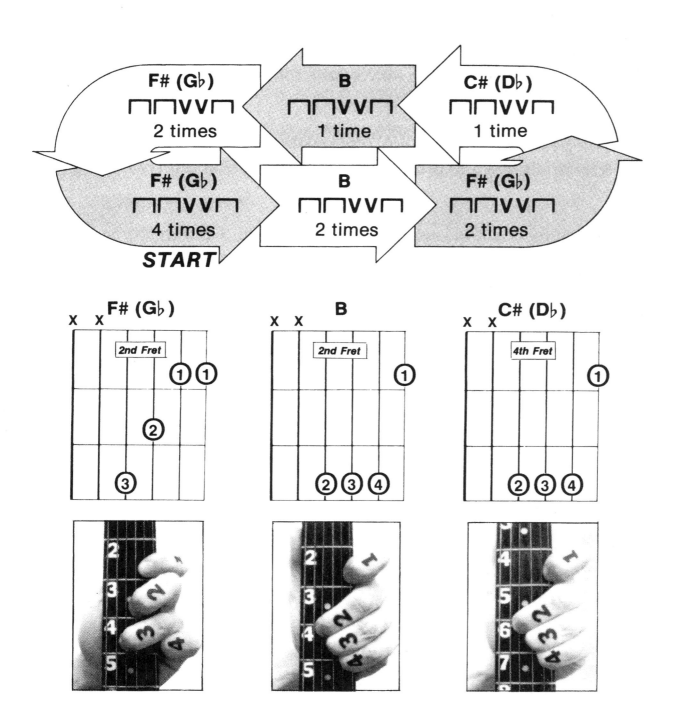

So far you have been shown the **A, D, G, E, F, A#** or **B♭**, **D#** or **E♭**, **F#** or **G♭** progessions. The remainder of the 12 progressions are presented to you on the rock group cards at the back of your book.

When trying to discover which one of the 12 basic progressions goes with a particular rock song you should remember that each rock song is unique in certain respects.

1) The basic **12 progressions** offer a **wide range for your voice.** You should choose the progression that you feel comfortable singing with.

2) Sometimes a rock song may use a basic 3 chord progression, however, the **order that the 3 chords are played** in the song **may vary.**

3) Strum patterns and **timing often varies from song to song.** The most common strum pattern has been chosen for the purpose of practicing the following progressions.

Student Notes

FORMING A ROCK BAND

The remainder of this book will show you how to play the same 12 progressions you have just learned on different positions of the guitar. Why??

Playing a progression on a **different position** of the guitar gives the progression a **slightly different sound.**

When a band is using a progression, **each band member** should **play the progression** on a **different place** on the guitar in order to **create a variety of sound.**

This approach also gives you, as an individual, the opportunity to learn how to play the **same chords** on **different places on the guitar.**

Student Notes

All of the chords that we have used so far can be found on various positions on the guitar.

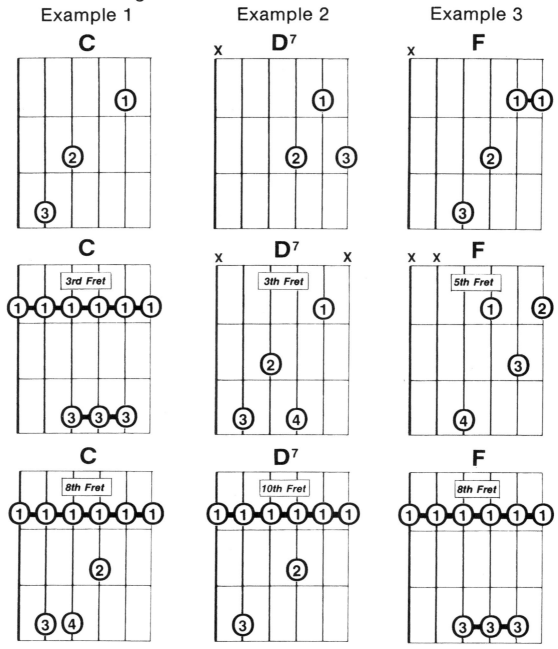

From the examples shown above you can see that the **same chord** may be **played at different places on the guitar** thereby giving it a slightly different sound. We will now study the 12 progressions placed on different positions of the guitar.

PLAYING OUR BASIC 3 CHORD PROGRESSIONS ON THE BASS STRING CHORDS

We will play our **progressions** using **bass chords. Bass chords** are chords that are **played on** the **4th, 5th,** and **6th strings of the guitar.** The progression has a deeper, fuller sound if you use bass chords instead of those chords played in the beginning of the book.

A (Bass Chord)

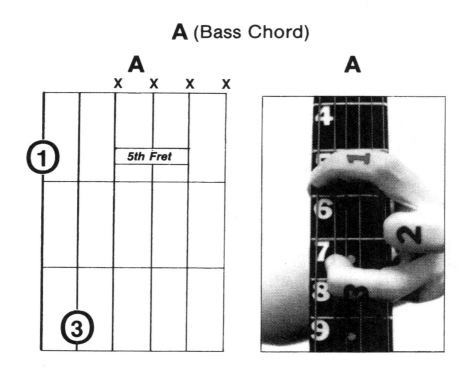

1) To play the **A** bass chord you must put your **1st finger** on the **5th fret** of the **6th string** while placing **3rd finger** on the **7th fret** of the **5th string.**

2) When playing bass chords you should only strike the strings that your fingers are on. When playing the **A bass** chord you should only **strike** the **5th** and **6th strings.**

1) You should play the entire 8 strums as many times as indicated underneath each strum pattern.

2) These **down strums** should be **played** with **very short, fast strokes.**

3) You should be able to play the entire strum pattern in 2 taps of your foot.

(A) Bass Chord Progression

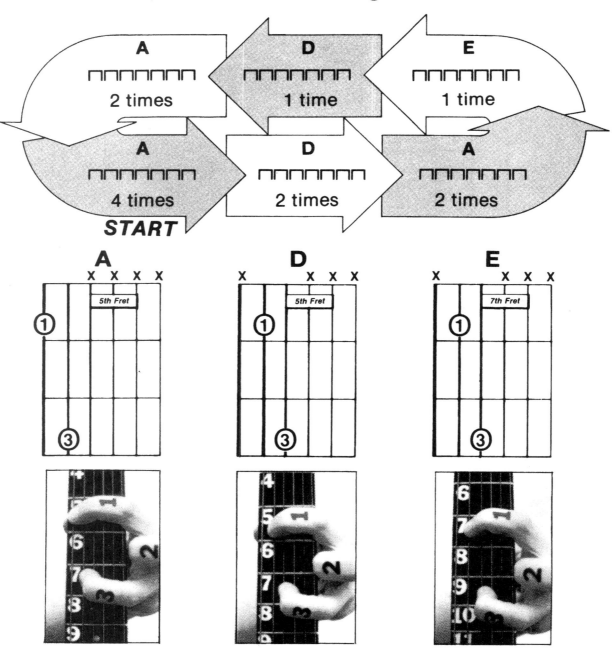

The G Progression (Bass Chords)

1) Remember **don't stop between chord changes.**

2) Only strike the two strings your fingers are on.

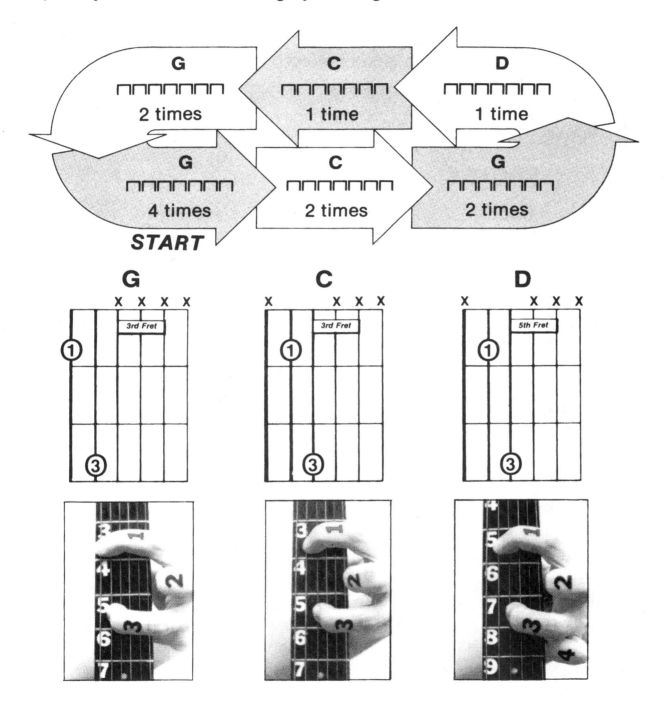

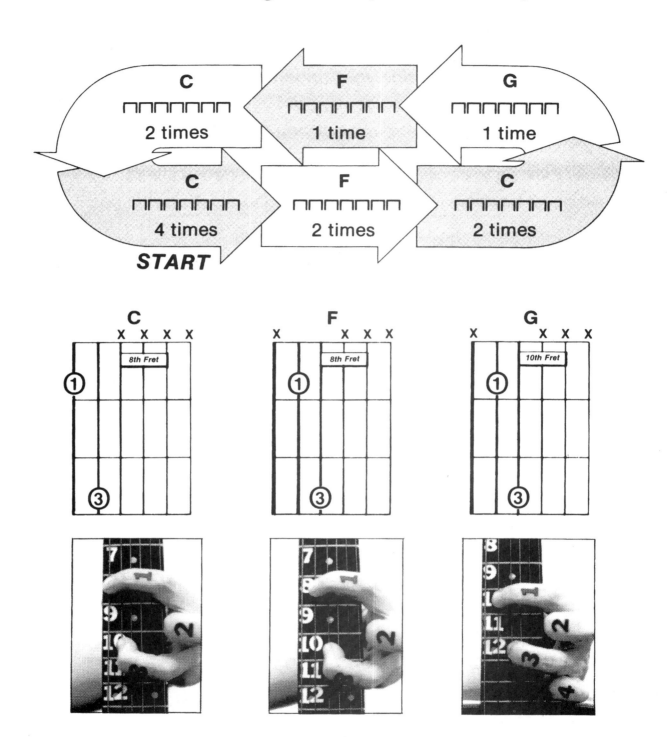

The other nine progressions are shown on the rock group cards in the back of the book.

BASS CHORDS WITH ADDED NOTES

We can also play our 12 progressions of **bass chords** with **added notes.** The added note will give the bass chords you have just learned a rock sound common to many songs.

C (bass chord)

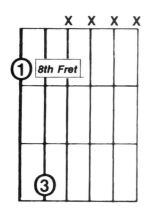 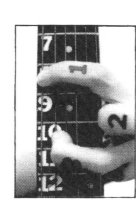

C (add A)

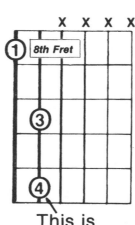 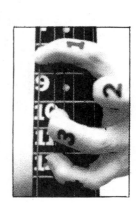

This is
the added
A note.

C (bass chord)

To play the **C** bass chord you should put your **1st finger** on the **8th fret** of the **6th string** and your **3rd finger** on the **10th fret** of the **5th string.**

C (add A)

To play **C (add A)** you leave your **1st finger** on the **8th fret** of the **6th string.** You should **lift** up your **3rd finger** from the **10th fret** of the **5th string** and **place** your **4th finger** on the **12th fret** of the **5th string. Lifting up your 3rd finger will allow you to stretch your 4th finger further.**

1) The strum pattern is 3 ⊓ strums. For the **1st** and **2nd strums** you should **play** the **C bass chord** while on the **3rd** ⊓ **strum** of the strum pattern you should **play the C (add A).**

2) All three ⊓ strums of the strum pattern should be played within one tap of your foot.

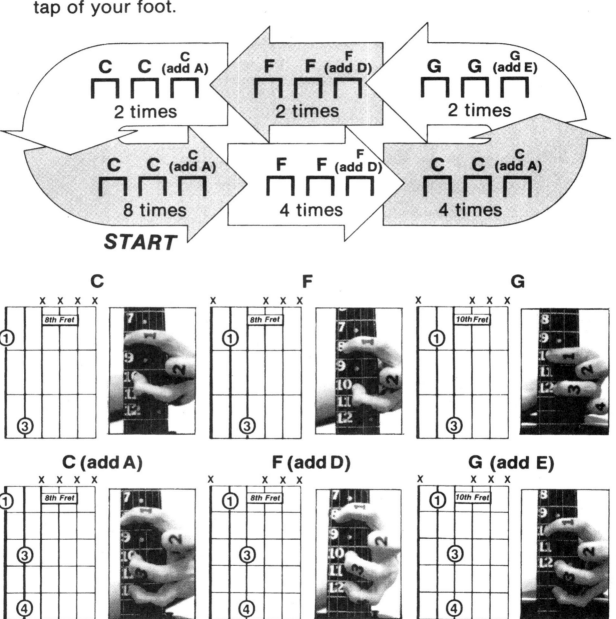

The G Bass Progression (Added Note)

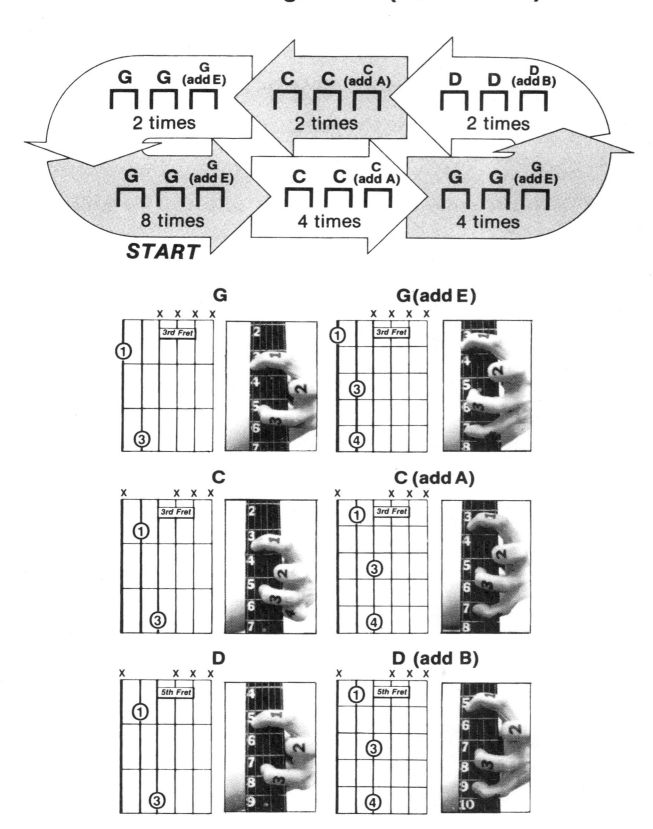

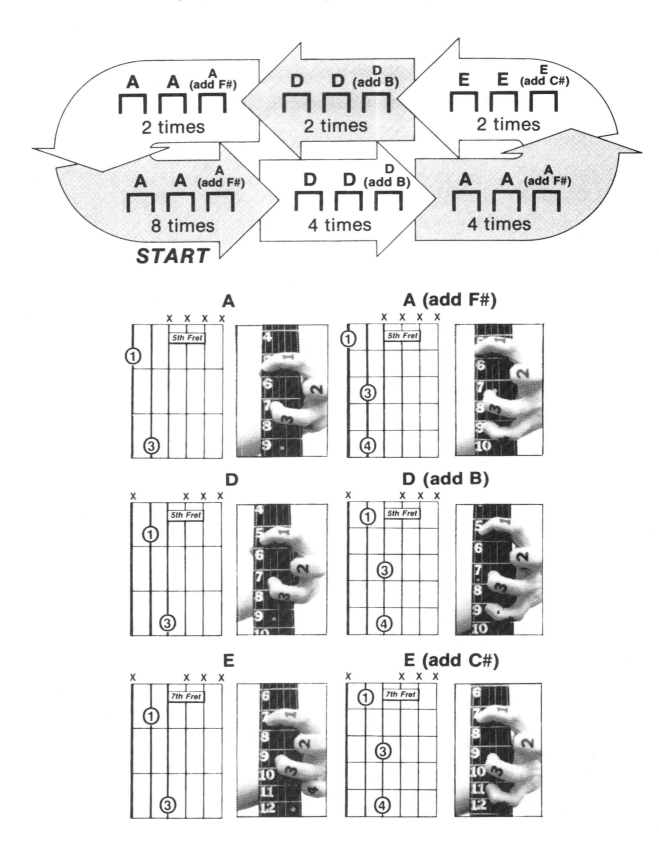

The B Bass Progression (Added Note)

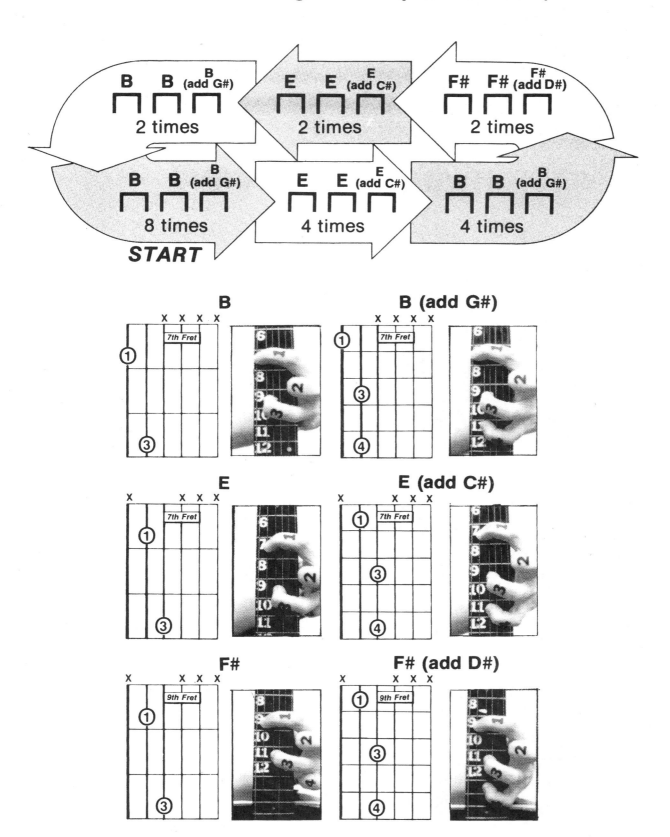

The remainder of the bass progressions (added notes) not shown here are shown on the rock cards at the back of the book.

In order to play a full bar chord you must use your first finger to press down on all six strings. Playing a **full bar chord** is preferable since it **may be moved up and down the neck of the guitar.** In addition, the full bar chord has a fuller, more powerful sound than other chords.

TWO FULL BAR FORMS

Form 1

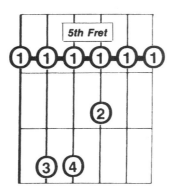 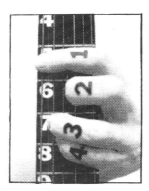

Form 2

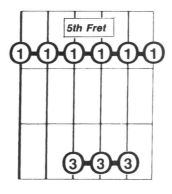 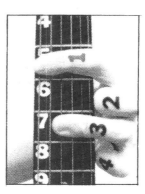

1) These forms may be moved up and down the neck of the guitar.

2) Let us begin with Form 1 and place it on the 5th fret. On the **5th fret Form 1** is an **A chord.** A full explanation of how to play the **A** chord is on the following pages.

The (A) Major Chord

We will study the full bar form on the 5th fret. The full bar form as played on the 5th fret is an **A** major chord (A).

You must be thinking, **"How am I ever going to press down all six strings with one finger?"** It's really not as hard as it looks. Here are some helpful hints.

To play **A** your **1st finger** must **bar all six strings** on the **5th string.** Your **2nd finger** should be on the **6th fret** of the **3rd string.** Your **3rd finger** should be on the **7th fret** of the **5th string** and your **4th finger** should be on the **7th fret** of the **4th string.**

The Right Way   The Wrong Way

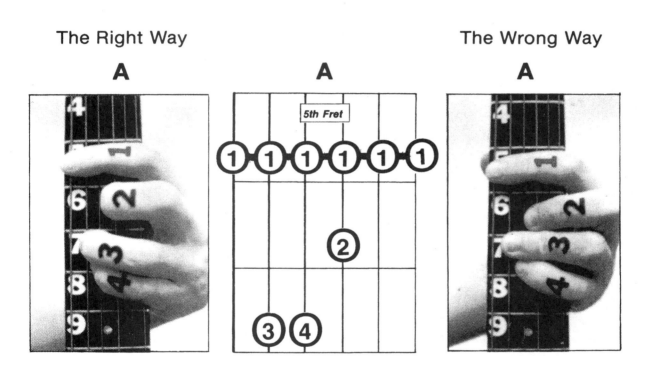

Your fingers should be up straight. If you bend your fingers over, you will get a thud (unclear sounds).

Your fingers are bent over touching other strings, causing unclear sounds.

A great deal of time should be spent on this particular chord. As soon as you are able to play this chord, the other bar chords will be much easier to play.

Pressure Points for the (A) Chord

Pressure from your 1st finger should be directed at these points.

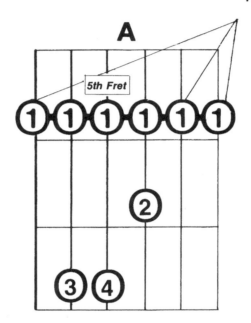

1) You should press down on all 6 strings with your 1st finger.

2) As you can see from the diagram above, you only have to concentrate on pressing down with your 1st finger on 1st, 2nd, and 6th strings.

3) You should apply pressure with your 2nd, 3rd and 4th fingers on the 3rd, 4th and 5th strings.

The D Major Chord

We will now study Form 2 on the 5th fret. **Form 2** played on the **5th fret** is a **D** chord. Practice this chord until all the strings make a clear sound.

To play **D** your **1st finger** must bar (press down) **all six strings** on the **5th fret.** Your **3rd finger** should bar the **2nd, 3rd,** and **4th strings** on the **7th fret.**

Pressure from your first finger should be directed at these points.

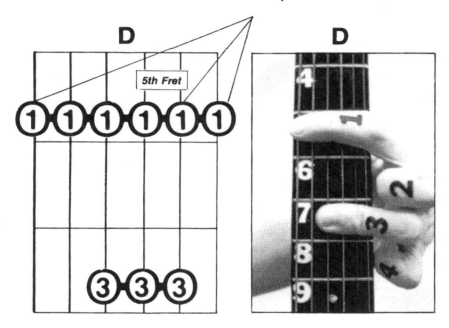

This bar position is the most difficult for most people. With time and practice you will be able to play this chord.

PLAYING OUR BASIC PROGRESSIONS
USING FULL BAR CHORDS

By moving our two forms up and down the neck of the guitar we will be able to **play all of our 12 basic progressions.**

The (A) Progression (Full Bar Chord)

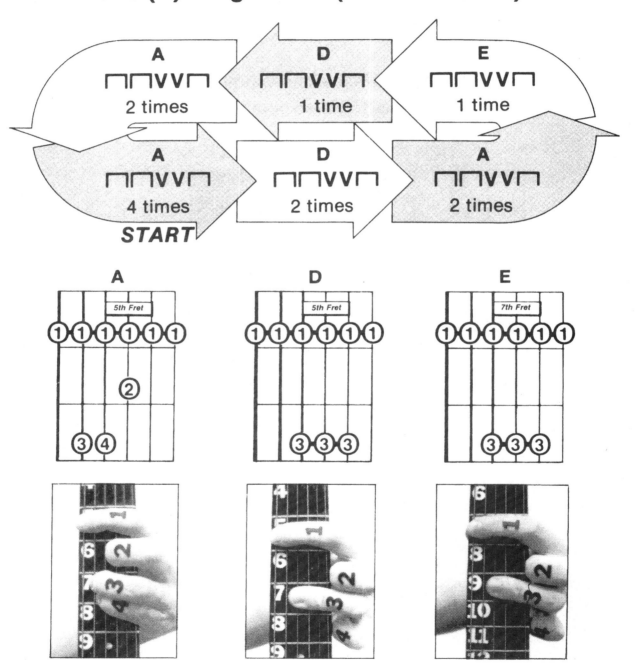

The C Progression
(Full Bar Chords)

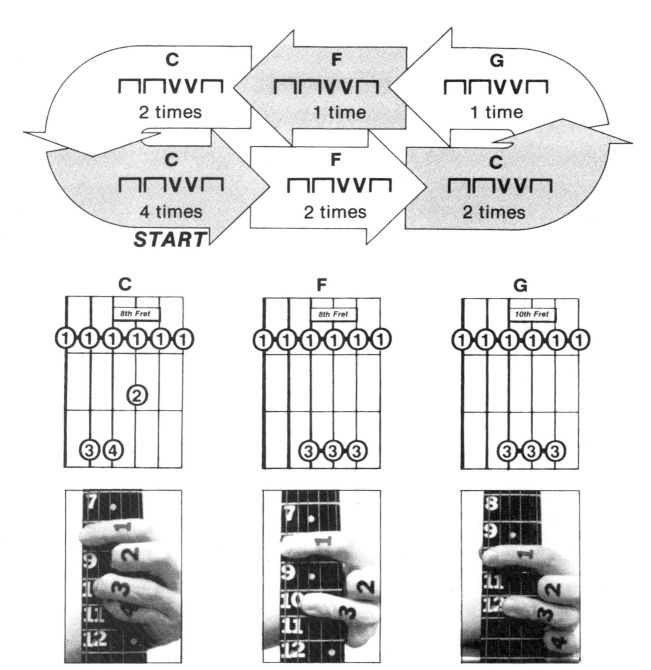

The G Progression
(Full Bar Chords)

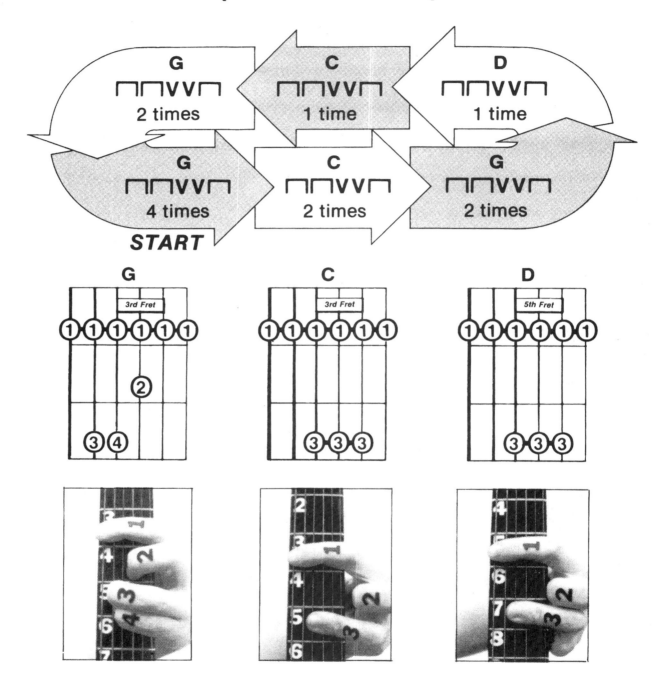

The G# Or A♭ Progression
(Full Bar Chords)

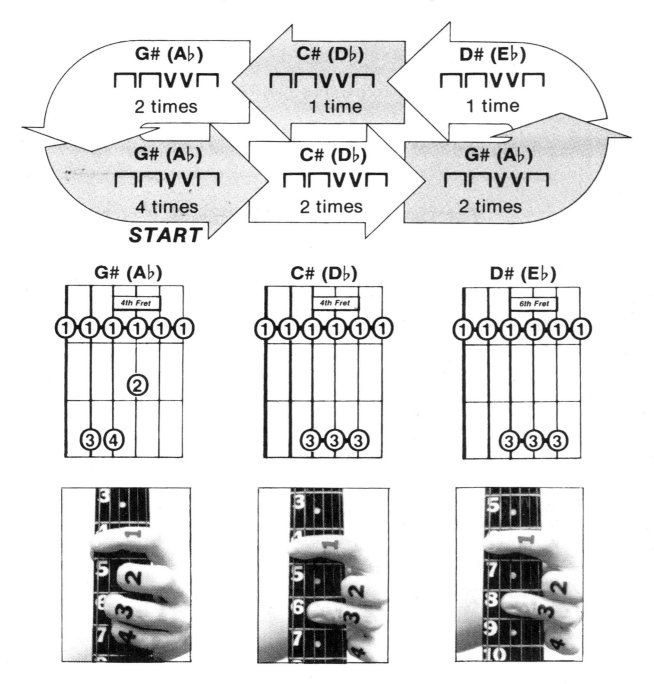

The rock group cards in the back of the book show you how to use full bar chords for the remainder of the twelve progressions.

Individual Use

1) **Choose** the **progression** that **sounds best** with your **voice.**

2) **Play the song** through while **trying** each of the **four parts** shown on the rock cards.

3) **Choose the part** that you think **sounds best** with **your song.**

For Use As Rock Group Charts

1) **Choose** the **progression** that **sounds best** with **your voices.**

2) **Cut** the progression chart you have chosen into **four parts. Give each member** of the group a **different part.**

3) **Play** the song having **each group** member **play his part.**

4) **Your group** will be **playing** the **same progression** in **four parts.**

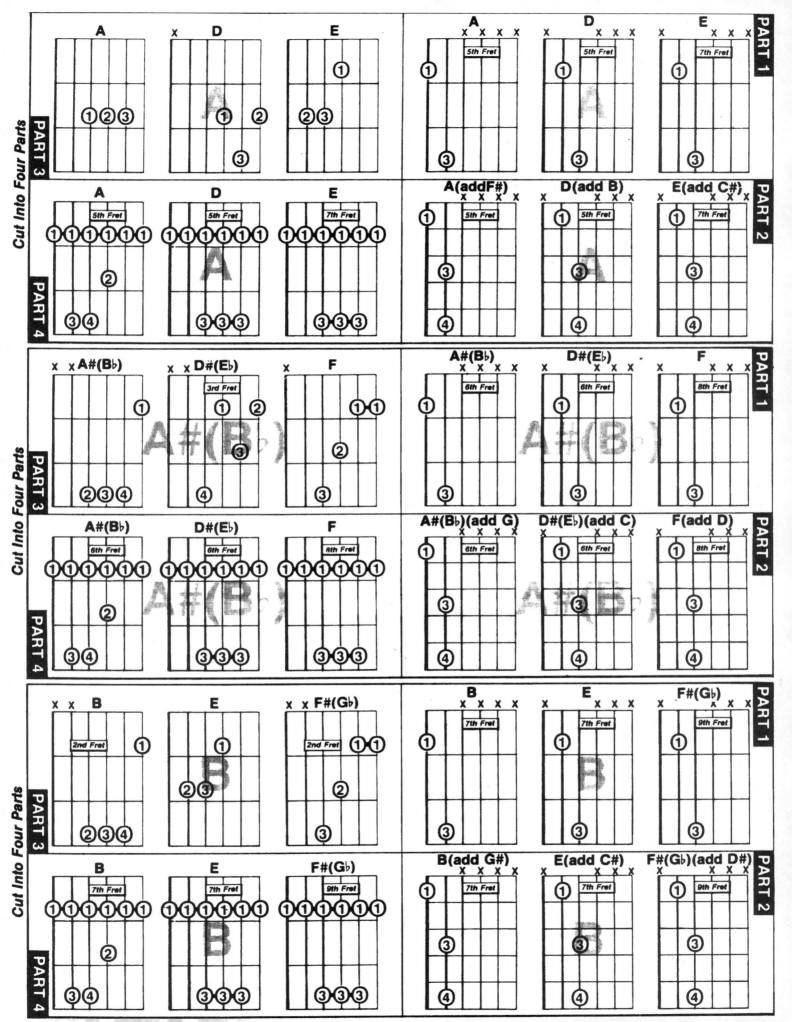

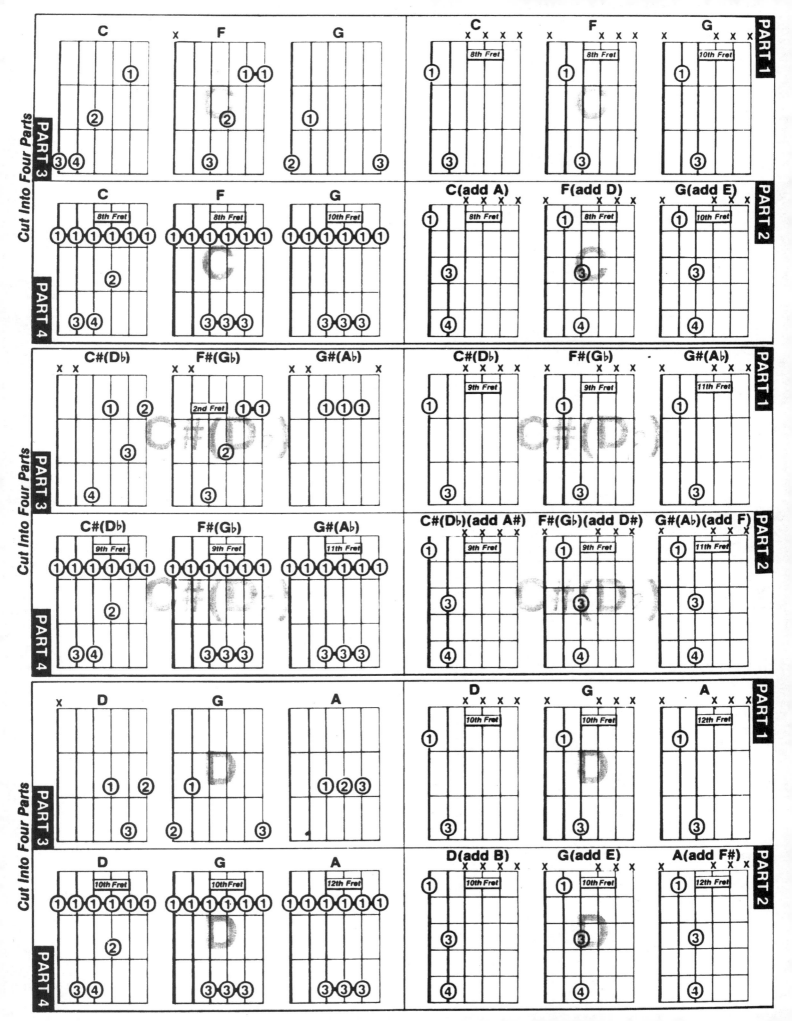

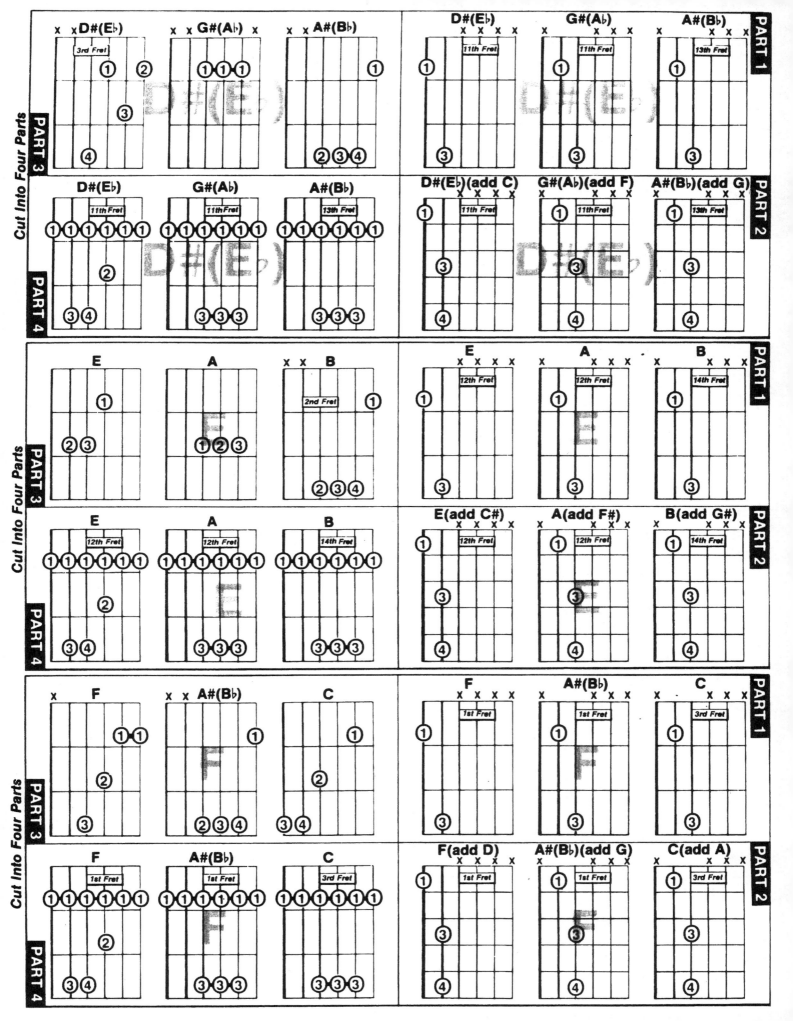

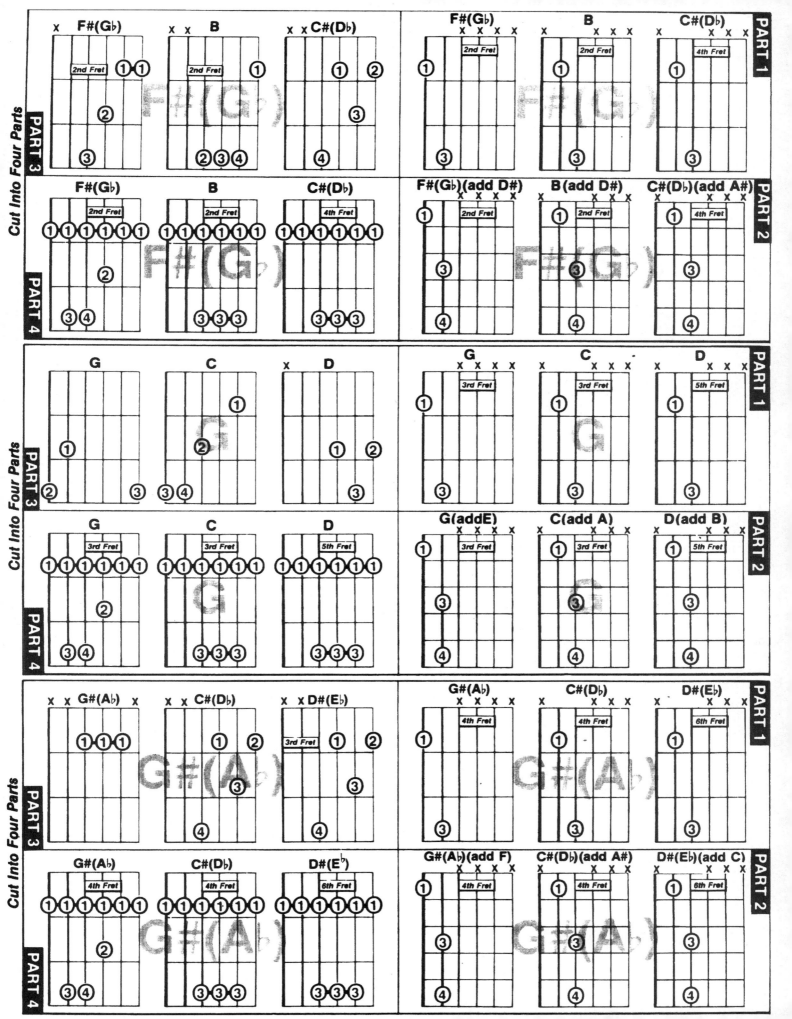